United States
Department of
Agriculture

Forest Service

Southern
Research Station

General Technical
Report SRS–118

Ozone Injury Across the Southern United States, 2002–06

Anita K. Rose and John W. Coulston

Authors

Anita K. Rose is an Ecologist and **John W. Coulston** is a Supervisory Research Forester with the Forest Inventory and Analysis Research Work Unit, U.S. Forest Service, Southern Research Station, Knoxville, TN 37919.

Cover photos: Sweetgum, sassafras and yellow-poplar, three species known to be sensitive to ozone-induced foliar injury. Cover photos courtesy of Paul Wray, Iowa State University, Bugwood.org (yellow-poplar); and Chris Evans, River to River CWMA, Bugwood.org (sweetgum and sassafras).

August 2009

Southern Research Station
200 W.T. Weaver Blvd.
Asheville, NC 28804

Ozone Injury Across the Southern United States, 2002–06

Anita K. Rose and John W. Coulston

Abstract

In the Eastern United States, hourly concentrations of ozone typically range from 30 to 50 parts per billion (ppb), with events that may exceed 100 ppb. Typical exposure levels can cause visible foliar injury to some plant species and have the potential to reduce tree growth by up to 10 percent per year, depending on species and environment. As part of the Forest Service, U.S. Department of Agriculture, Forest Inventory and Analysis (FIA) Program, ozone-induced foliar injury is evaluated in the South between late July and mid-August on about 350 ozone biosites. For 2002 through 2006, ozone injury occurred on between 8 (2006) and 29 percent (2003) of the sampled biosites. South Carolina had the highest percentage of biosites with injury in 3 out of 5 years. The area at greatest risk from ozone injury occurred in northern Georgia. Both the moisture index and the combination of ozone exposure and moisture were significantly different for biosites where injury was observed and biosites where injury was not observed. This evidence suggests that, despite reported declines in ambient ozone concentrations over the past 10 years, some forest areas in the South were classified in the low and no risk categories due to the moisture deficit conditions that existed during the 2002-06 time period. The correlation between ozone injury and moisture conditions, as well as the consistent low to moderate levels of injury, occurring year after year in some parts of the South, warrant continued monitoring and close scrutiny for potential forest health impacts. FIA conducts the only annual nationwide systematic survey for ozone-induced foliar injury. This information is extremely valuable to research on trends in ozone exposure and injury and the impacts to vegetation across the United States.

Keywords: Biomonitoring, FIA, forest health, indicator species, ozone.

CONTENTS

Ozone Injury Across the Southern United States, 2002–06

Anita K. Rose and John W. Coulston

Highlights

Biomonitoring of ozone injury by FIA from 2002 through 2006 in the South found the following:

- Ozone injury occurred on between 8 (2006) and 29 percent (2003) of the biosites sampled.

- South Carolina had the highest percentage of biosites with injury in 3 out of 5 years.

- Foliar injury occurred most frequently on blackberry (*Rubus allegheniensis*), milkweed (*Asclepias*), and sweetgum (*Liquidambar styraciflua*).

- Both the moisture index (MI) and the combination of ozone exposure and moisture were significantly different (p < 0.001) for biosites where injury was observed and biosites where injury was not observed.

- An estimated 17.5 million acres of forest land and 20.4 billion cubic feet of susceptible tree volume were classified in the low, moderate, and high risk categories.

- The area at greatest risk from ozone injury occurred in northern Georgia.

- Most of the forest area in the South was classified in the low or no risk categories.

Introduction

In the Eastern United States, hourly ambient concentrations of ozone typically range from 30 to 50 parts per billion (ppb), with events that may exceed 100 ppb (Chappelka and Samuelson 1998, U.S. Environmental Protection Agency 2004, U.S. Environmental Protection Agency 2008). Typical exposure levels can cause visible foliar injury to some plant species and have the potential to reduce tree growth by up to 10 percent per year, depending on species and environment (Chappelka and Samuelson 1998). Ozone is the product of

chemical reactions that take place in the lower atmosphere when volatile organic compounds (VOCs) mix and react with nitrogen oxides (NO_x) in the presence of sunlight. Anthropogenic emissions, primarily from the combustion of organic compounds (i.e. gasoline and coal), account for a large majority of NO_x inputs to the environment (fig. 1). In contrast, VOCs come primarily from natural sources, such as trees and other vegetation, although some of the total inputs of VOCs do come from industrial and vehicular emissions. Weather plays a key role in the formation of ozone, with hot, dry, calm, cloudless days providing ideal conditions for VOCs and NO_x to combine and react to form ozone (U.S. Environmental Protection Agency 2004).

Ozone exposure, uptake, and sensitivity all play important roles in the response of plants to ozone. Ozone exposure varies spatially and temporally. Weather patterns and changes in emissions of precursors account for a majority of year to year variations. Between 1970 and 2003, the VOC and NO_x emissions that contribute to the formation of ground-level ozone decreased 54 percent and 25 percent, respectively (U.S. Environmental Protection Agency 2004).

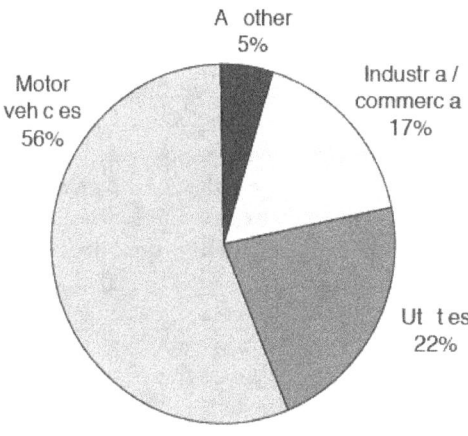

Figure 1—NO_x emissions by source category

Spatially, ozone exposure varies by topography, with higher elevations often having higher concentrations than lower, and more exposed sites having higher ozone than sheltered sites (Anderson and others 1988, Samuelson and Kelly 2001). In addition, ozone concentrations are typically higher in open areas than within closed forests. Within forests, ozone concentrations are higher in the upper canopy than the lower, with lowest concentrations on the forest floor (Fredericksen and others 1995, Samuelson and Kelly 2001).

The uptake of ozone by plants depends upon many things, including physiological age, climate, and light availability. Instantaneous uptake rates of ozone tend to be higher in seedlings than mature trees, although cumulative uptake is higher in mature trees than in seedlings (Fredericksen and others 1995). Additionally, higher light availability in the upper canopy means higher ozone uptake than in the lower canopy. Site characteristics and available moisture also factor into the variability of ozone uptake (Bartholomay and others 1997, Peterson and others 1993, Samuelson and Kelly 2001). Dry conditions tend to decrease stomatal conductance, thereby lowering ozone uptake (Patterson and others 2000). However, there is some evidence that ozone can exacerbate drought stress in some trees by reducing root growth (Bartholomay and others 1997, McLaughlin and Downing 1996).

Sensitivity to ozone varies by species, genotype, physiological age, and leaf morphology. Several species, such as black cherry (*Prunus serotina*) and blackberry (*Rubus allegheniensis*), are known to be sensitive to ozone and exhibit a visible foliar response. There is some evidence that sensitivity can vary by genotype within a given species, with resistant strains showing little or no response compared to sensitive ones (Benoit and others 1982). This, in effect, could lead to reduced genetic diversity with sensitive strains being outcompeted by more resistant ones. Physiological age can also alter sensitivity, with seedlings being less sensitive to ozone than mature trees (Samuelson and Edwards 1993), although the reverse may be true for some species (Fredericksen and others 1995). Leaf morphology can alter the sensitivity of leaves on a given plant, with shade leaves being more sensitive than sun leaves, although, as noted, ozone concentrations tend to be higher in the upper canopy than the lower. In addition to the visible foliar injury exhibited by some species, reduced growth and decreased species richness have been reported from studies of ozone impacts to plants (Arbaugh and others 1998, Barbo and others 1998, Bartholomy and others 1997, McLaughlin and Downing 1996, Rebbeck 1996, Reinert and others 1996, Samuelson and Edwards 1993, Somers and others

1998). However, the effect of ozone on forest health is not fully understood due to the lack of studies showing direct relationships between foliar injury, uptake, and physiological response (Fredericksen and others 1995, Somers and others 1998). Further confounding the ozone injury issue are the uncertainties surrounding the extrapolation of responses from controlled studies of seedlings to large forest trees (Samuelson and Kelly 2001). A review of the impacts of ozone on trees, including issues surrounding scaling tree-level responses to the landscape to determine ozone-induced effects, can be found in Bytnerowicz (2002), Chappelka and Samuelson (1998), Karnosky and others (2007), and Samuelson and Kelly (2001).

The objectives of this report are to: (1) describe ozone injury observed on Forest Inventory and Analysis (FIA) ozone biomonitoring sites from 2002 through 2006, (2) quantify ambient ozone concentrations from 2002 through 2006, (3) describe moisture conditions from 2002 through 2006, and (4) perform a risk assessment to elucidate areas at high risk of ozone impacts.

Methods

Study Area

The study area for our analysis was an 11 State region in the South including Alabama, Arkansas, Florida, Georgia, Kentucky, Louisiana, North Carolina, South Carolina, Tennessee, Texas, and Virginia (fig. 2). Parts of Florida and Texas were excluded due to a lack of suitable biomonitoring locations and insufficient suitable species. Ozone injury data were not collected in Mississippi or Oklahoma during the 2002–06 time period. In addition, ozone injury data were not collected in Louisiana in 2006.

Field Methods

As part of the Forest Service, U.S. Department of Agriculture FIA Program, ozone-induced foliar injury in the South is evaluated by field personnel between late July and mid-August (U.S. Department of Agriculture 2004). Ozone biomonitoring sites (biosites) are determined by using a national ozone triangular grid, separate from the regular FIA triangular plot grid. This grid allows for more closely spaced biosites in areas of higher potential ozone exposure (fig. 2). Within each cell of the grid, an ozone biosite is established using a set of criteria, such as access, size, and number of species (table 1).

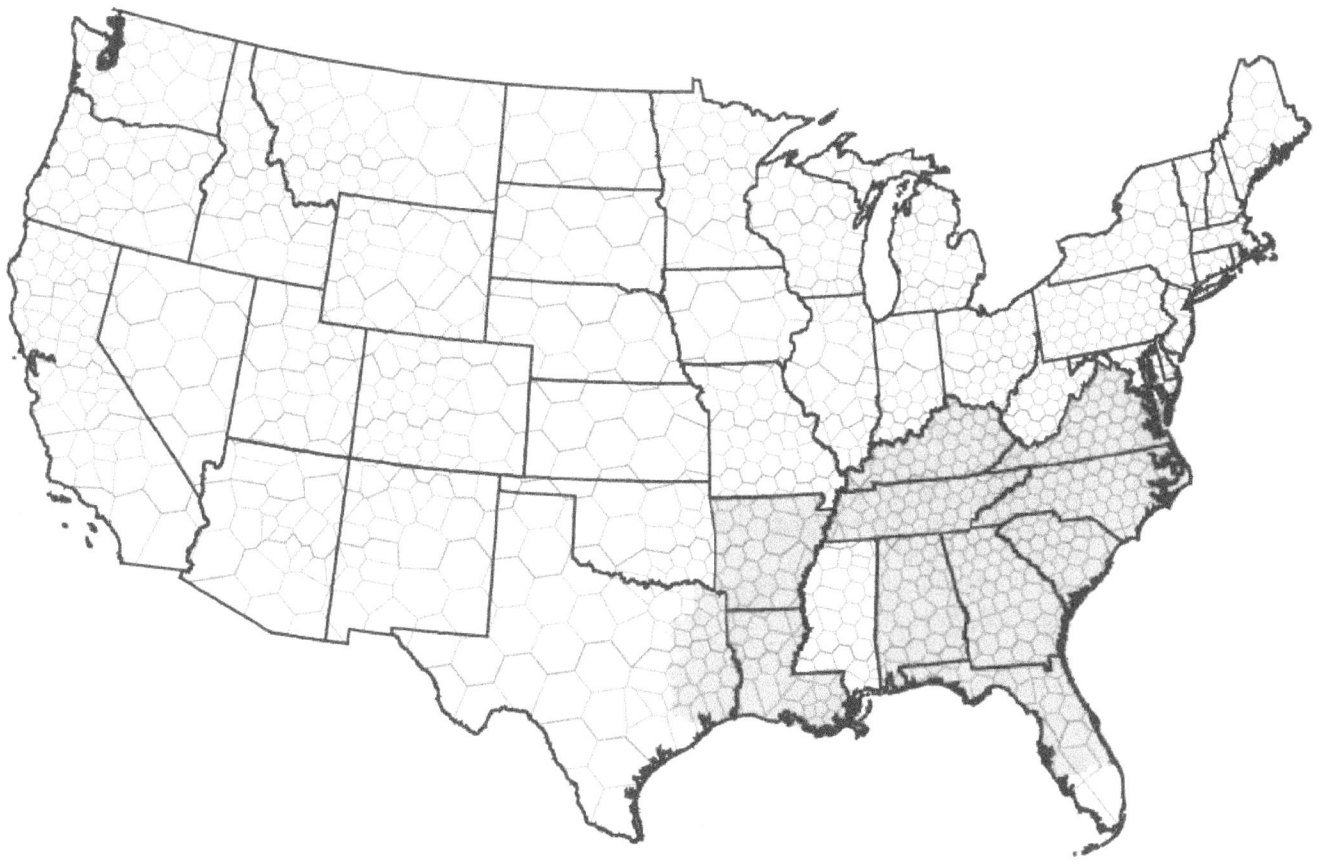

Figure 2—Ozone biomonitoring program sampling polygons and study area (shaded), 2002–06. The intrastate borders for the shaded areas in Texas and Florida are the county boundaries.

Table 1—Site selection criteria for ozone injury assessments

Site	First choice[a]	Second choice
Access	Easy	Easy
Location	Single location is used	Two locations within 3 miles of each other, preferably with similar site conditions
Size of opening	>3 acres (1.2 ha); wide open area; <50 percent crown closure	Between 1 to 3 acres; long, narrow, or irregularly sized opening
Species count	More than three species	Two or more species
Plant count	30 plants of 3 species; 10 to 30 plants of additional species	30 plants of 2 species; 10 to 30 plants of additional species
Soil conditions	Low drought potential; good fertility	Moderately dry; moderate fertility
Site disturbance	No recent (1 to 3 years) disturbance; no obvious soil compaction	Little or no disturbance; no obvious soil compaction

[a] Best site.

Once a biosite is established, at least 30 individuals of at least 2, preferably 3 or more, bioindicator species are examined for ozone injury (table 2). The key characteristic of bioindicator plants is that they respond to ambient levels of ozone with distinct foliar symptoms that are easy to diagnose. For example, bioindicator species, such as yellow-poplar (*Liriodendron tulipifera)* and sweetgum (*Liquidambar styraciflua*), exhibit an upper surface foliar injury symptom that can be readily distinguished from other foliar injuries (fig. 3). While ozone bioindicator species are considered highly sensitive, there can be variability among and within ozone bioindicator species. This is why 30 observations from each of at least 2 bioindicator species are required, while 3 or more is preferable (82 percent of biosites between 2002 and 2006 had 3 or more species evaluated). Each plant is examined for amount of injury (percentage of leaves on a plant with injury) and severity (percentage of leaf area of injured leaves with ozone injury). For injury validation purposes, field personnel then collect three symptomatic leaves for each individual species at each biosite.

Analyses

Biosite index—For each biosite, a biosite index (BI) was calculated based upon the average score (amount as a proportion multiplied by severity as a proportion) for each species (the species index) averaged across all species on the biosite and then multiplied by 1,000 to allow categories to be defined by integers (Smith and others 2003). For mapping, interpretation, and risk analysis, the BI values were assigned to four categories based on Smith and others 2003 (table 3).

Table 3—Classification scheme for the FIA ozone biosite index

Injury category	Biosite index	Bioindicator response	Risk assumption
1	0–4.9	Little or no injury	No risk
2	5.0–14.9	Light to moderate injury	Low risk
3	15.0–24.9	Moderate to severe injury	Medium risk
4	≥25	Severe foliar injury	High risk

Ozone exposure—The Environmental Protection Agency (EPA) monitors hourly ambient ozone concentrations at 266 locations distributed across the study area. We obtained these data as well as data for the surrounding States from the EPA for 2002–06. We then used the SUM06 index to summarize each ozone season. The SUM06 index is a commonly used method to summarize ambient ozone concentrations for a particular time period of interest (see Davis and Orendovici 2006 for example). It is the sum of all hourly ozone concentrations ≥ 0.06 parts per million (ppm). For our application we calculated the SUM06 index for a 12-hour period (8 a.m. to 8 p.m.) for June, July, and August for each year. Any monitoring station that had > 25 percent missing hourly observations was removed and monitoring stations that had ≤ 25 percent missing observations were adjusted based on EPA guidelines. We then created interpolated surfaces for SUM06 for each year using inverse distance squared weighting based on the 12 nearest neighbors. We then summarized the land area in each of four classes (The H. John Heinz III Center for Science, Economics, and the Environment 2008) by year for comparison. The classes were: SUM06 ≤ 10, 10 < SUM06 ≤ 20, 20 < SUM06 ≤ 30, SUM06 > 30 ppm-hours per year.

Table 2—Ozone bioindicator species for the Eastern United States

Type	Common name	Scientific name[a][b]
Tree species		
	White ash	*Fraxinus americana* L.
	Sweetgum	*Liquidambar styraciflua* L.
	Yellow-poplar	*Liriodendron tulipifera* L.
	Pin cherry	*Prunus pensylvanica* L. f.
	Black cherry	*P. serotina* Ehrh.
	Sassafras	*Sassafras albidum* (Nutt.) Nees
Herbaceous species		
	Spreading dogbane	*Apocynum androsaemifolium* L.
	Common and tall milkweed	*Asclepias* spp. L.
	Bigleaf aster	*Eurybia macrophylla* (L.) Cass.
	Allegheny blackberry	*Rubus allegheniensis* Porter

[a] Little (1979).

[b] USDA Natural Resources Conservation Service (2006).

(A) Yellow-poplar

(B) Black cherry

(C) Blackberry

Figure 3—Ozone injury symptoms on (A) yellow-poplar (photo courtesy of U.S. Forest Service, Region 8, Bugwood.org), (B) black cherry, and (C) blackberry (B and C photos courtesy of Gretchen Smith).

Moisture index—To examine the potential moisture available to plants from 2002 to 2006 within our study area we used a moisture index (MI) based on precipitation and potential evapotranspiration (PET) (Akin 1991, Coulston and Riitters 2005, Koch and others, in press). Parameter-elevation Regression on Independent Slopes (PRISM) climate mapping system data served as the basis for these maps. The PRISM system is knowledge-based, integrating

a localized climate-elevation regression function with other algorithmic components: station weighting, topographic facets, coastal proximity, and a two-layer atmosphere (Daly and others 2002). In the case of precipitation, the PRISM product was used directly. PET was calculated using Thornthwaite's (1948) model as described in Akin (1991). The PRISM temperature data was used to implement Thornthwaite's model. We then used a modified MI

(Willmott and Feddema 1992) to examine the ratio of precipitation to PET, which bounds the ratio between -1 and 1.

$$MI = \begin{cases} P/PET-1, & P < PET \\ 1-PET/P, & P \geq PET \\ 0, & P = PET = 0 \end{cases}$$

where

MI = Moisture index
P = Precipitation
PET = Potential evapotranspiration measure in the same units as P

We calculated MI for June, July, and August for each of the 5 years (2002–06). We then summarized the land area in each of three classes, corresponding to moisture deficit (MI $\leq$ -0.15), approximate moisture balance (-0.15 < MI $\leq$ 0.15), and moisture surplus (MI > 0.15) by year for comparison.

Integration of injury, exposure, and moisture—To examine the potential relationship among ozone induced foliar injury, ambient ozone, and moisture we overlayed the biosites with the SUM06 maps and MI maps. We then used Hotelling's T^2 test and 95 percent Bonferroni simultaneous confidence intervals (Johnson and Wichern 2002) to examine potential significant differences in mean response vectors between biosites without injury (BI = 0) and those with injury (BI > 0). The null hypothesis was

$$H_0 = \left(\overline{\frac{SUM06_i}{MI_i}} \right) - \left(\overline{\frac{SUM06_0}{MI_0}} \right) = \begin{pmatrix} 0 \\ 0 \end{pmatrix}$$

where

$_i$ = biosites with injury
$_0$ = biosites without injury

Hotelling's test is a common multivariate statistical technique which accounted for the correlation between ambient ozone concentrations and the MI (r = 0.62). When using these tests we had to account for the fact that the ozone biomonitoring survey is not an equal probability sample. To accomplish this, each observation was weighted proportional to the area of the polygon from figure 2 where the biosite resides. Biosites that represent more land area

were weighted more heavily than those that represented less land area. Also, because the MI and the SUM06 index were measured on different scales, we standardized each variable to a mean of zero and a variance of one.

Risk assessment—Foliar injury is surveyed to determine where negative impacts to forest trees may be occurring. Monitoring foliar injury of bioindicator plants does not identify specific levels of ozone present, but rather identifies whether conditions were favorable for ozone injury to occur (Coulston and others 2003). Although correlations between high levels of ozone exposure and foliar injury have been observed (Hildebrand and others 1996, Smith and others 2003), strong relationships between ozone exposure and tree responses have been difficult to confirm (Chappelka and Samuelson 1998).

In order to develop risk assessment maps and evaluate the likelihood of ozone injury to forests, biosite indices were spatially interpolated using inverse distance squared weighting, a standard interpolation technique by which ozone risk is modeled for all unmeasured locations utilizing weighted averages from measured biosites (Smith and others 2007). The 5 yearly maps were then averaged to create the 5-year map of ozone risk. Averaging of biosite scores over a period of several years gives a clearer picture of the potential for foliar injury in a given location. Overlaying this map with FIA data allowed us to estimate the volume of sensitive tree species at risk of ozone injury and the area of forest land at risk of ozone injury using the standard FIA compilation methods presented in Bechtold and Patterson (2005). Each tree species measured on each FIA forest mensuration plot (FIA plot) was assigned a sensitivity ranking (sensitive, moderately sensitive, insensitive, or unknown) based on the literature review provided by Smith and others (2007).

Results

Biosites

Every year over the 5-year study period, between 26,695 and 30,897 bioindicator plants on 316 to 359 biosites were evaluated for ozone-induced foliar injury. The number of biosites with ozone-induced foliar injury varied between 27 (8 percent) in 2006 and 93 (29 percent) in 2003 (table 4). In 2002 and 2003 between 5 and 6 percent of biosites were in categories 3 and 4, while in 2004 and 2006 only about 1 percent of biosites were in categories 3 and 4 (table 5). In every year except 2006, South Carolina had foliar injury

Table 4—Number of evaluated biosites with ozone-induced foliar injury by year and State

State	2002	2003	2004	2005	2006
			number		
Alabama					
Evaluated	25	32	32	34	34
Injured	0	0	0	3	0
Arkansas					
Evaluated	25	25	24	24	24
Injured	0	4	6	0	0
Florida					
Evaluated	18	22	23	23	23
Injured	1	0	0	0	0
Georgia					
Evaluated	45	45	45	45	45
Injured	15	19	10	13	0
Kentucky					
Evaluated	31	29	23	37	38
Injured	10	17	9	3	4
Louisiana					
Evaluated	21	21	21	20	—
Injured	0	0	0	0	—
North Carolina					
Evaluated	42	29	46	46	46
Injured	10	14	10	6	14
South Carolina					
Evaluated	29	30	30	26	26
Injured	14	17	16	14	4
Tennessee					
Evaluated	39	37	40	40	40
Injured	7	13	5	4	3
Texas					
Evaluated	17	18	28	25	21
Injured	3	1	0	0	0
Virginia					
Evaluated	24	32	39	39	38
Injured	1	8	5	0	2
Total					
Evaluated	316	320	351	359	335
Injured	61	93	61	43	27

— = no sample for the cell.

Table 5—Number and percentage of biosites in each biosite index category in the South, by year

Injury category[a]		2002	2003	2004	2005	2006
1	Number	282	270	331	328	326
	Percent	89.2	84.4	94.3	91.4	97.3
2	Number	17	32	16	15	6
	Percent	5.4	10.0	4.6	4.2	1.8
3	Number	8	8	2	6	2
	Percent	2.5	2.5	0.6	1.7	0.6
4	Number	9	10	2	10	1
	Percent	2.8	3.1	0.6	2.8	0.3

[a] For corresponding biosite index values, response, and risk assumptions see table 3.

on 48 to 57 percent of biosites. South Carolina also had the highest percentage of biosites with injury in 2002, 2004, and 2005. In 2003 and 2006, Kentucky and North Carolina, respectively, had the highest percentage of biosites with injury. In 2002, 2003, and 2005 South Carolina had the highest percentage of biosites in categories 3 and 4 (table 6). In 2004 and 2006, Arkansas and Kentucky, respectively, had the highest percentage of biosites in categories 3 and 4. Florida, Louisiana, and Texas did not have any biosites in category 2 and higher in any year. Alabama and Arkansas did not have any biosites in category 2 or higher in 4 out of 5 years.

In Georgia and South Carolina, the distribution of biosites with injured plants was fairly consistent from year to year, with the exception of 2006 (figs. 4 through 8). Injury was typically detected near Columbia and the Greenville-Spartanburg area, and sometimes along the coast in South Carolina. In Georgia, the injury often occurred in areas surrounding Atlanta, Athens, and Macon. In North Carolina, ozone injury was often detected surrounding the Charlotte and Winston-Salem areas. The injury detected in Virginia typically occurred in the coastal region, and in the southwest portion of the State. Very often there was a line of injury in northwest Kentucky, around Lexington and Louisville, that in some years extended down to the northwest corner of Tennessee (as in 2003), or to the northeast corner of Arkansas (as in 2004). Another area with injury occurred in east Tennessee. In 2003 this area extended from Chattanooga northward along the border with North Carolina into southwest Virginia. A similar pattern existed in 2005, although with less injury and without the

Table 6—Percentage of biosites by injury category, year, and State

Year and State	Injury category[a]				Year and State	Injury category[a]			
	1	2	3	4		1	2	3	4
	percentage					*percentage*			
2002					**2004 (continued)**				
Alabama	100.0	0.0	0.0	0.0	North Carolina	97.8	2.2	0.0	0.0
Arkansas	100.0	0.0	0.0	0.0	South Carolina	73.3	23.3	3.3	0.0
Florida	100.0	0.0	0.0	0.0	Tennessee	100.0	0.0	0.0	0.0
Georgia	82.2	11.1	2.2	4.4	Texas	100.0	0.0	0.0	0.0
Kentucky	87.1	6.5	3.2	3.2	Virginia	100.0	0.0	0.0	0.0
Louisiana	100.0	0.0	0.0	0.0					
North Carolina	85.7	7.1	4.8	2.4	**2005**				
South Carolina	69.0	10.3	6.9	13.8	Alabama	97.1	2.9	0.0	0.0
Tennessee	84.6	7.7	5.1	2.6	Arkansas	100.0	0.0	0.0	0.0
Texas	100.0	0.0	0.0	0.0	Florida	100.0	0.0	0.0	0.0
Virginia	95.8	4.2	0.0	0.0	Georgia	73.3	13.3	4.4	8.9
					Kentucky	97.3	2.7	0.0	0.0
2003					Louisiana	100.0	0.0	0.0	0.0
Alabama	100.0	0.0	0.0	0.0	North Carolina	93.5	0.0	4.3	2.2
Arkansas	100.0	0.0	0.0	0.0	South Carolina	57.7	15.4	7.7	19.2
Florida	100.0	0.0	0.0	0.0	Tennessee	92.5	7.5	0.0	0.0
Georgia	73.3	15.6	6.7	4.4	Texas	100.0	0.0	0.0	0.0
Kentucky	79.3	10.3	3.4	6.9	Virginia	100.0	0.0	0.0	0.0
Louisiana	100.0	0.0	0.0	0.0					
North Carolina	86.2	13.8	0.0	0.0	**2006**				
South Carolina	46.7	33.3	6.7	13.3	Alabama	100.0	0.0	0.0	0.0
Tennessee	81.1	16.2	2.7	0.0	Arkansas	100.0	0.0	0.0	0.0
Texas	100.0	0.0	0.0	0.0	Florida	100.0	0.0	0.0	0.0
Virginia	84.4	6.3	3.1	6.3	Georgia	100.0	0.0	0.0	0.0
					Kentucky	92.1	2.6	5.3	0.0
2004					Louisiana	—	—	—	—
Alabama	100.0	0.0	0.0	0.0	North Carolina	95.7	4.3	0.0	0.0
Arkansas	91.7	0.0	4.2	4.2	South Carolina	92.3	7.7	0.0	0.0
Florida	100.0	0.0	0.0	0.0	Tennessee	95.0	2.5	0.0	2.5
Georgia	91.1	6.7	0.0	2.2	Texas	100.0	0.0	0.0	0.0
Kentucky	78.3	21.7	0.0	0.0	Virginia	100.0	0.0	0.0	0.0
Louisiana	100.0	0.0	0.0	0.0					

— = no sample for the cell.

[a] For corresponding biosite index values, response, and risk assumptions see table 3.

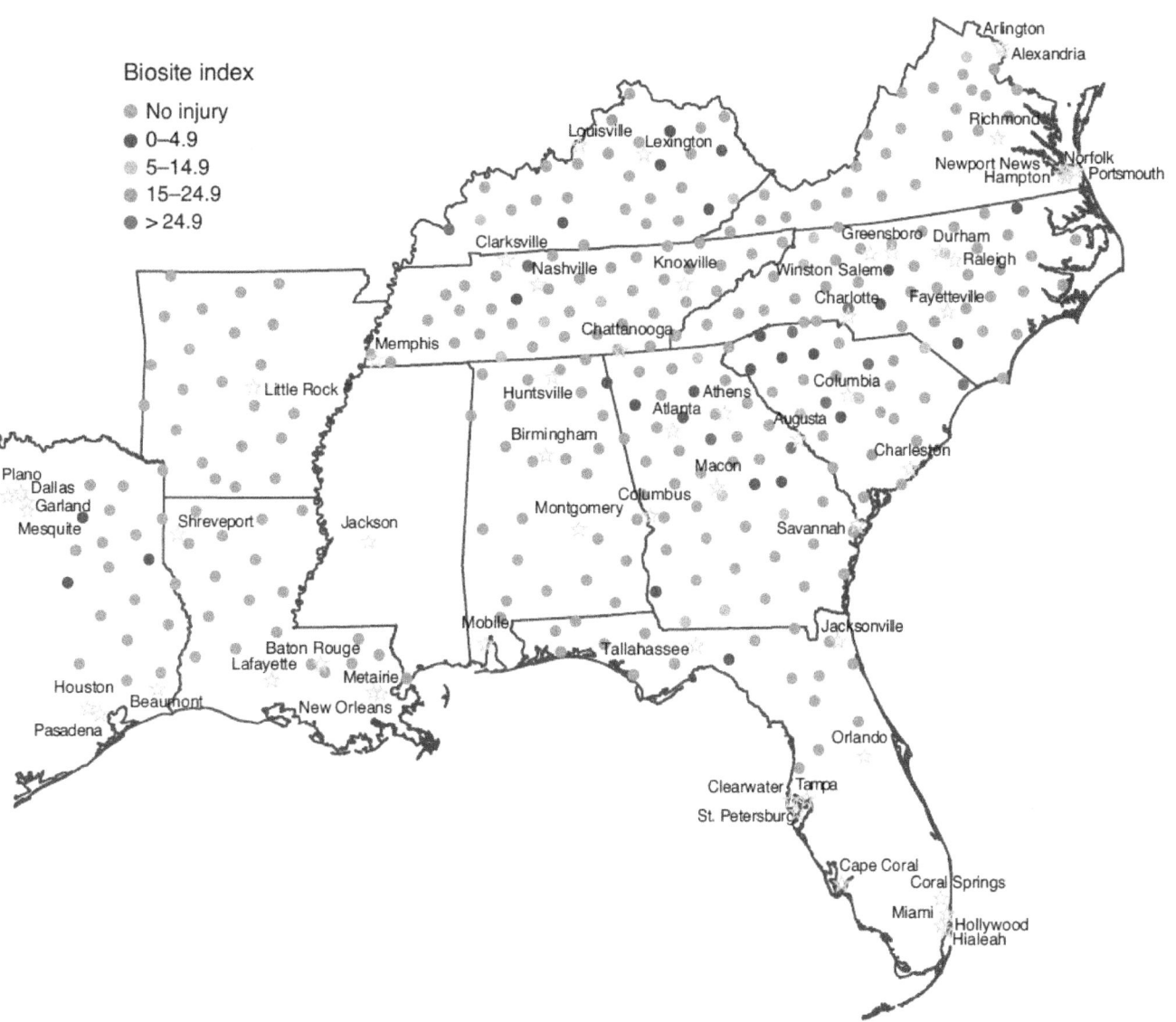

Figure 4—Ozone biosites and biosite index, 2002.

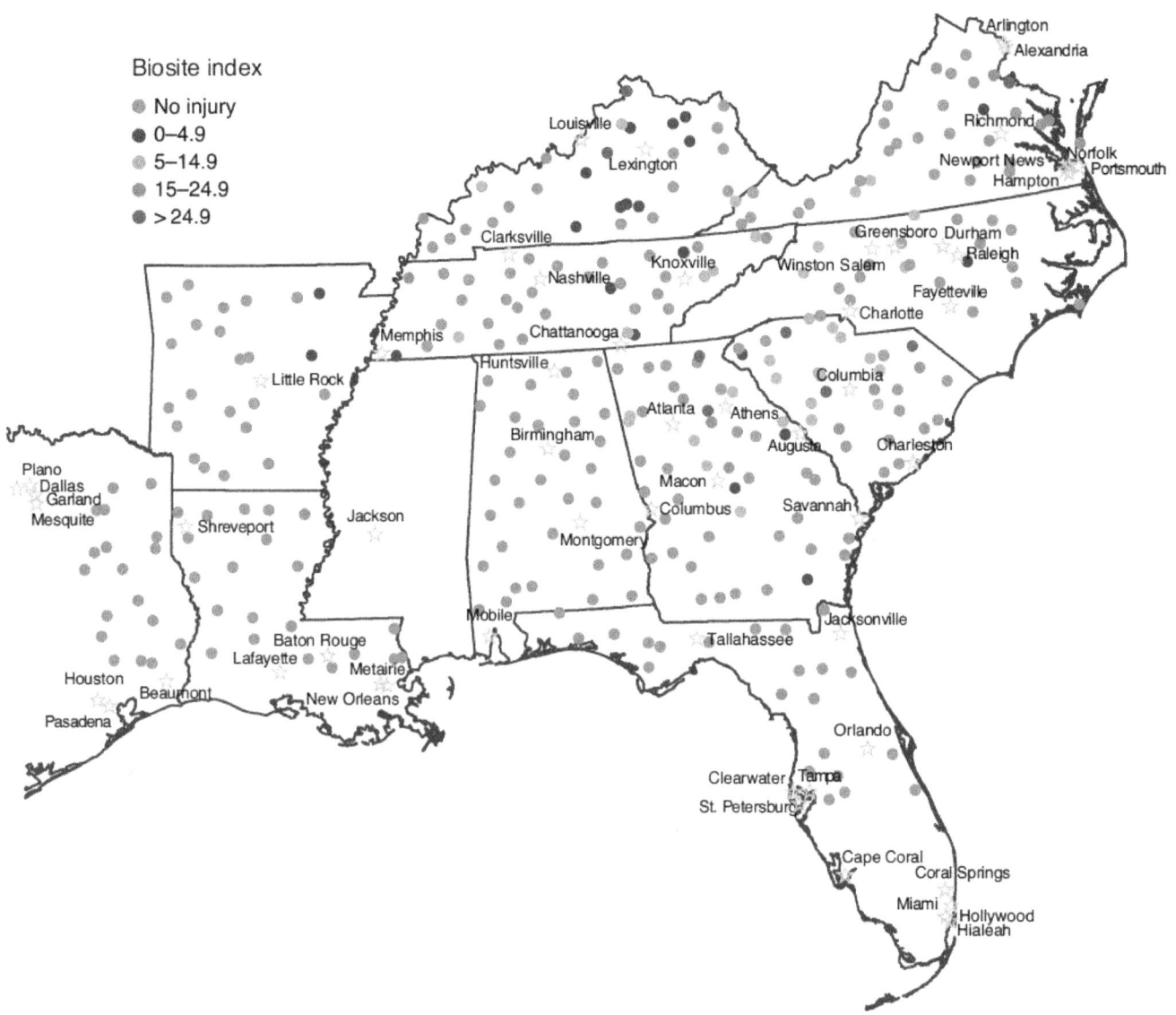

Figure 5—Ozone biosites and biosite index, 2003.

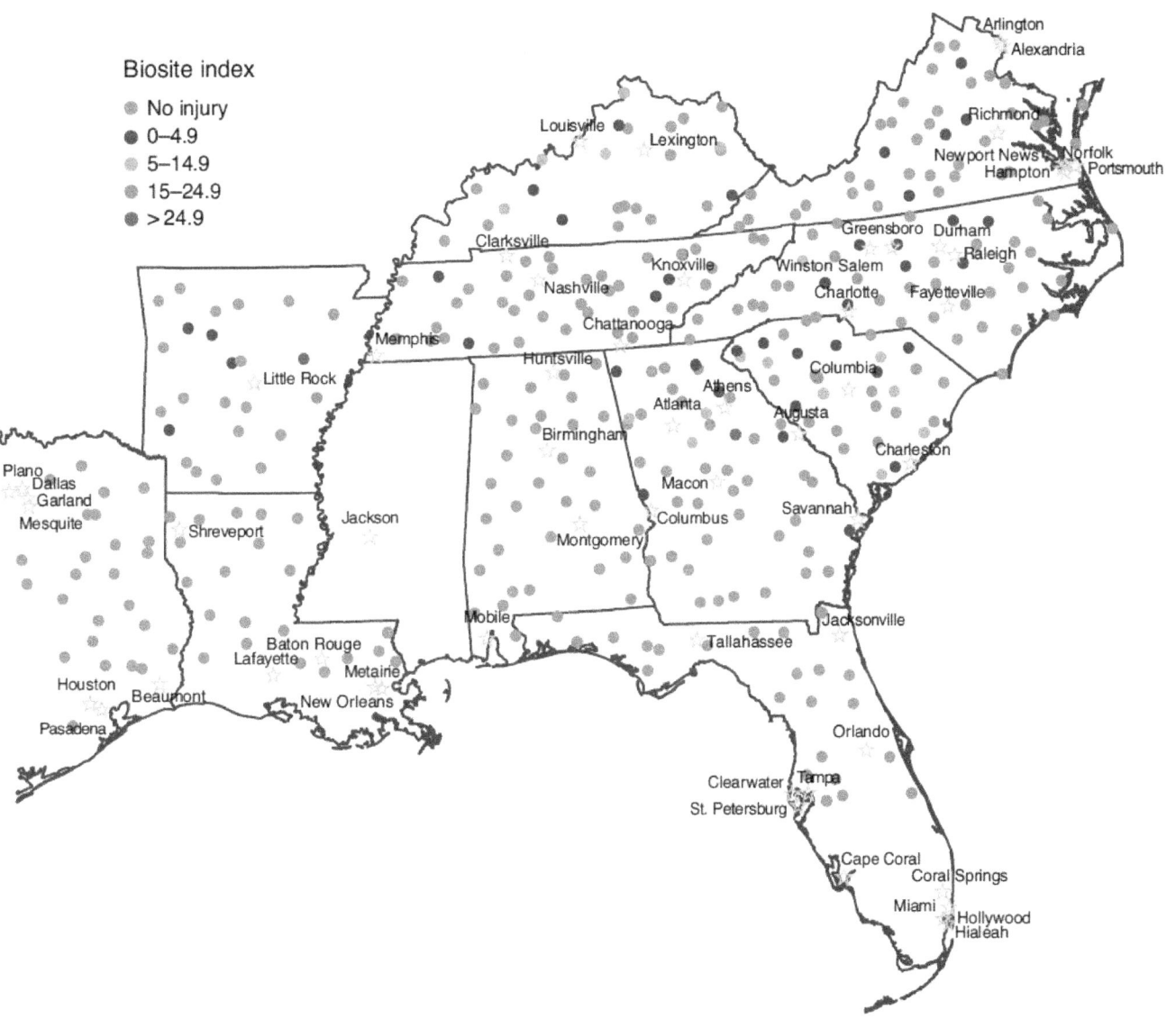

Figure 6—Ozone biosites and biosite index, 2004.

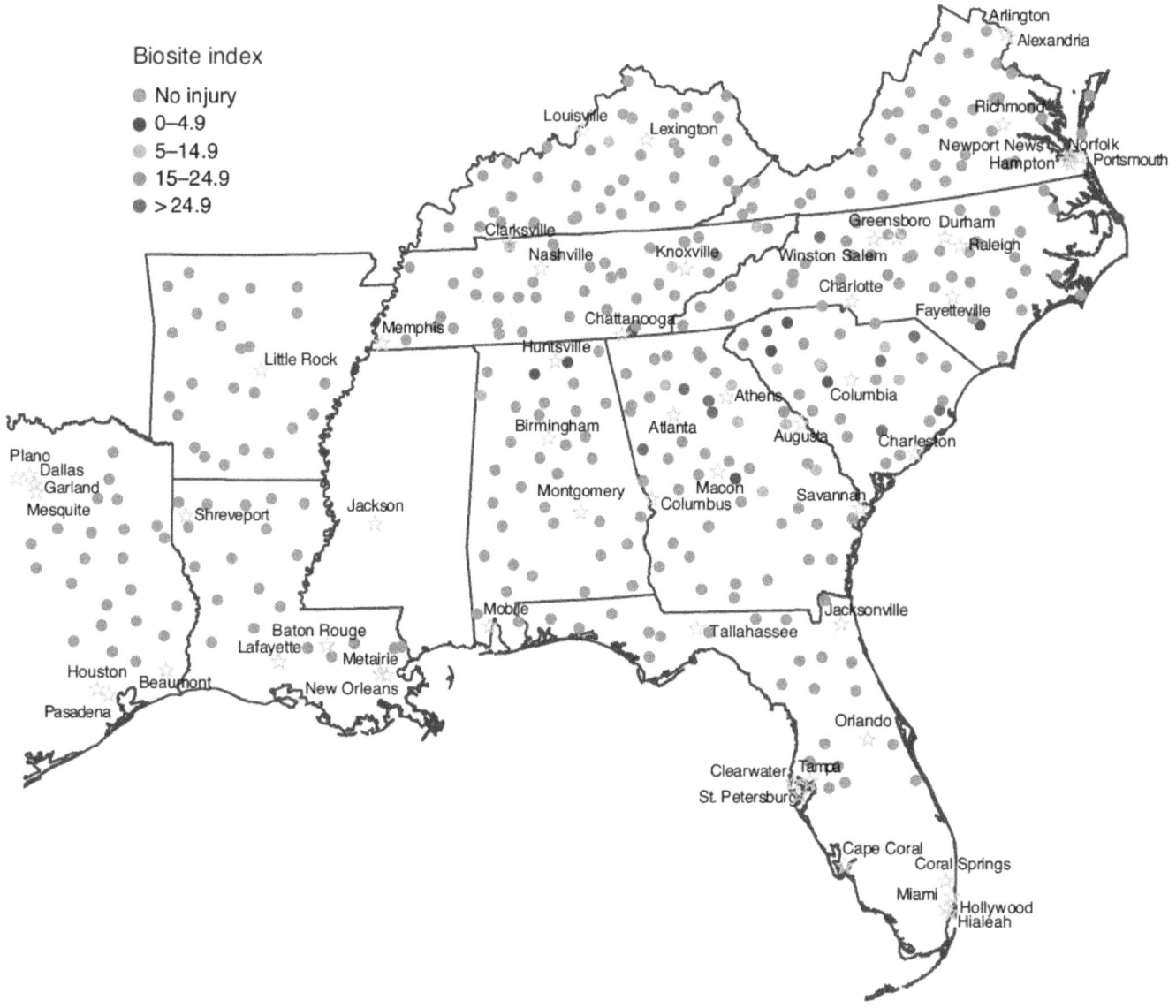

Figure 7—Ozone biosites and biosite index, 2005.

extension into southwest Virginia. The relatively small amount of injury that was detected in Arkansas occurred in the northeastern portion of the State, as in 2003 and 2004.

Bioindicators

Although the percentage of biosites with injury was relatively high in certain years and States, only between 1 percent and 3 percent of all evaluated plants had any injury (table 7). As was the case for biosites, the highest percentage

of plants with injury occurred in 2003 (3 percent), and the lowest in 2006 (0.6 percent). Ozone-induced foliar injury was found most frequently on blackberry, milkweed, and sweetgum. No injury was found in any year on big leaf aster (*Eurybia macrophylla*) or pin cherry (*Prunus pensylvanica*), but note the small sample size (table 7). Very little injury was found in any year on black cherry and sassafras (*Sassafras albidum*). In 2002, a year of relatively high injury, 6 percent of all evaluated sweetgum and 4 percent of all milkweed had injury. In 2003, another year of high

Figure 8—Ozone biosites and biosite index, 2006.

injury, 7 percent of all evaluated blackberry and 9 percent of all milkweed had injury. Blackberry had the highest 5-year average species index, followed by milkweed and sweetgum (fig. 9). Bioindicator species were not sampled equally. Blackberry and sweetgum accounted for over one-half of plants evaluated every year (fig. 10). In addition, species were not sampled equally across States. For example, in 2002, sassafras accounted for 31 percent of all plants evaluated for ozone injury in Texas; in Arkansas, however, it only accounted for 7 percent. Likewise, in 2004, sweetgum

accounted for 29 percent of plants evaluated in Alabama, but only for 7 percent in Kentucky.

Ozone Exposure

Ambient ozone concentrations in the South were interpolated to create a continuous surface and then summarized in four categories: SUM06 ≤ 10, 10 < SUM06 ≤ 20, 20 < SUM06 ≤ 30, SUM06 > 30 ppm-hours per year. The concentrations varied both spatially and temporally.

Table 7—Number of plants evaluated and injured by species and year

Species	Year				
	2002	2003	2004	2005	2006
	number[a]				
Big leaf aster					
Evaluated	10	12	30	30	—
Injured	0 (0%)	0 (0%)	0 (0%)	0 (0%)	—
Black cherry					
Evaluated	4,262	4,540	4,312	4,291	4,150
Injured	0 (0%)	24 (0.5%)	0 (0%)	4 (0.1%)	0 (0%)
Blackberry					
Evaluated	8,347	9,013	9,582	8,932	9,109
Injured	222 (2.7%)	659 (7.3%)	250 (2.6%)	269 (3.0%)	89 (1.0%)
Dogbane					
Evaluated	370	370	403	703	1,180
Injured	1 (0.3%)	6 (1.6%)	2 (0.5%)	0 (0%)	6 (0.5%)
Milkweed					
Evaluated	740	956	1,461	1,310	1,243
Injured	33 (4.5%)	90 (9.4%)	42 (2.9%)	8 (0.6%)	14 (1.1%)
Pin cherry					
Evaluated	—	—	352	70	30
Injured	—	—	0 (0%)	0 (0%)	0 (0%)
Sassafras					
Evaluated	2,714	3,245	3,298	3,413	2,598
Injured	4 (0.1%)	0 (0%)	0 (0%)	0 (0%)	0 (0%)
Sweetgum					
Evaluated	6,155	6,594	6,950	6,331	6,464
Injured	361 (5.9%)	40 (0.6%)	61 (0.9%)	46 (0.7%)	51 (0.8%)
White ash					
Evaluated	1,356	1,012	1,168	1,152	1,288
Injured	0 (0%)	19 (1.9%)	3 (0.3%)	0 (0%)	0 (0%)
Yellow-poplar					
Evaluated	2,741	3,234	3,341	3,005	3,009
Injured	7 (0.3%)	36 (1.1%)	5 (0.1%)	6 (0.2%)	1 (0.0%)
Total					
Evaluated	26,695	28,976	30,897	29,237	29,071
Injured	628 (2.4%)	874 (3.0%)	363 (1.2%)	333 (1.1%)	161 (0.6%)

— = no sample for the cell.

[a] Values in parentheses represent percentage of plants evaluated.

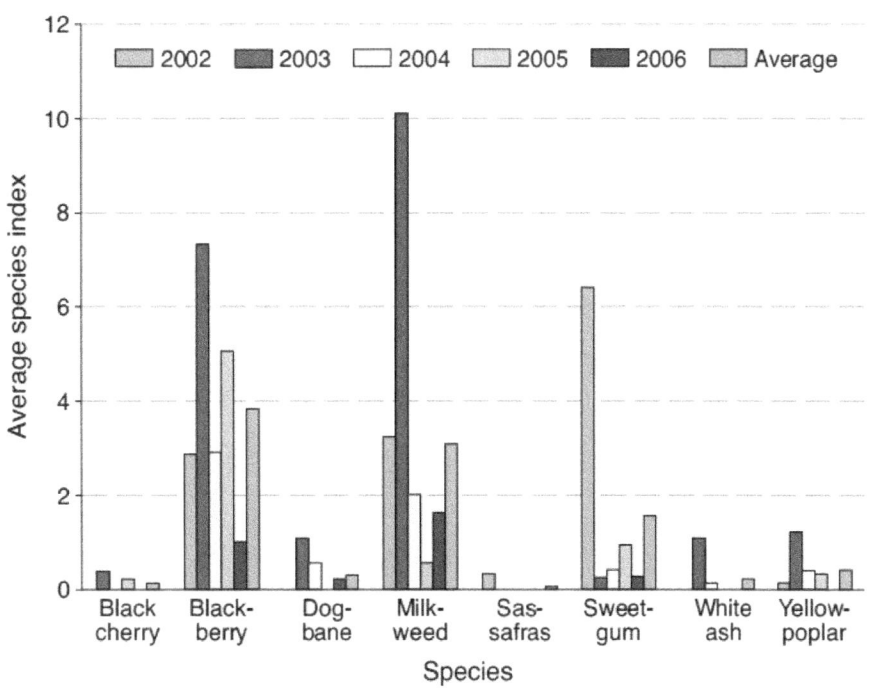

Figure 9—Average species index by year.

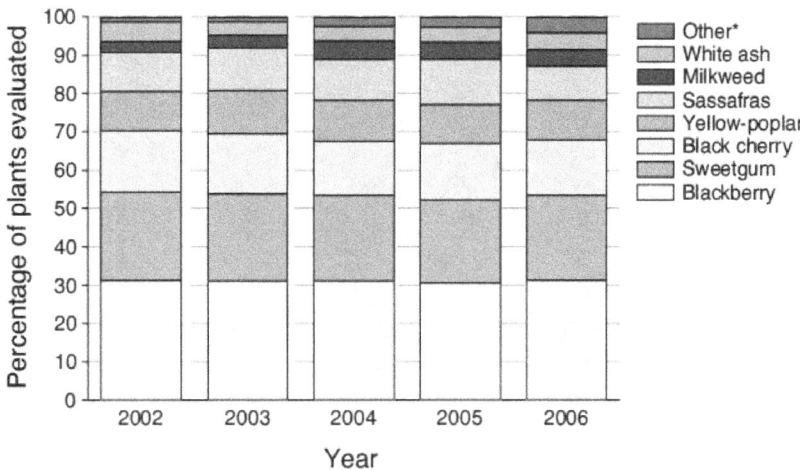

Figure 10—Percentage of plants evaluated each year represented by species. * Other = dogbane, pin cherry, and big leaf aster.

The highest average (2002–06) 3-month growing season SUM06 value was observed in North Carolina (fig. 11). Areas of relatively high SUM06 values (> 20 ppm-hours per year) were also observed in northern Georgia, east and west Tennessee, eastern Texas, east Arkansas, and through the piedmont of North Carolina and Virginia. Most of the land area in the South had average 3-month growing season SUM06 values < 20 ppm-hours per year. The lowest values of SUM06 were generally observed in Florida and Louisiana. However, there was temporal variation in the proportion of land in each category. In 2002, there were relatively equal amounts of land area in each category, which was in sharp contrast to 2004, when nearly 100 percent of the land area had concentrations < 20 ppm-hours per year (fig. 12).

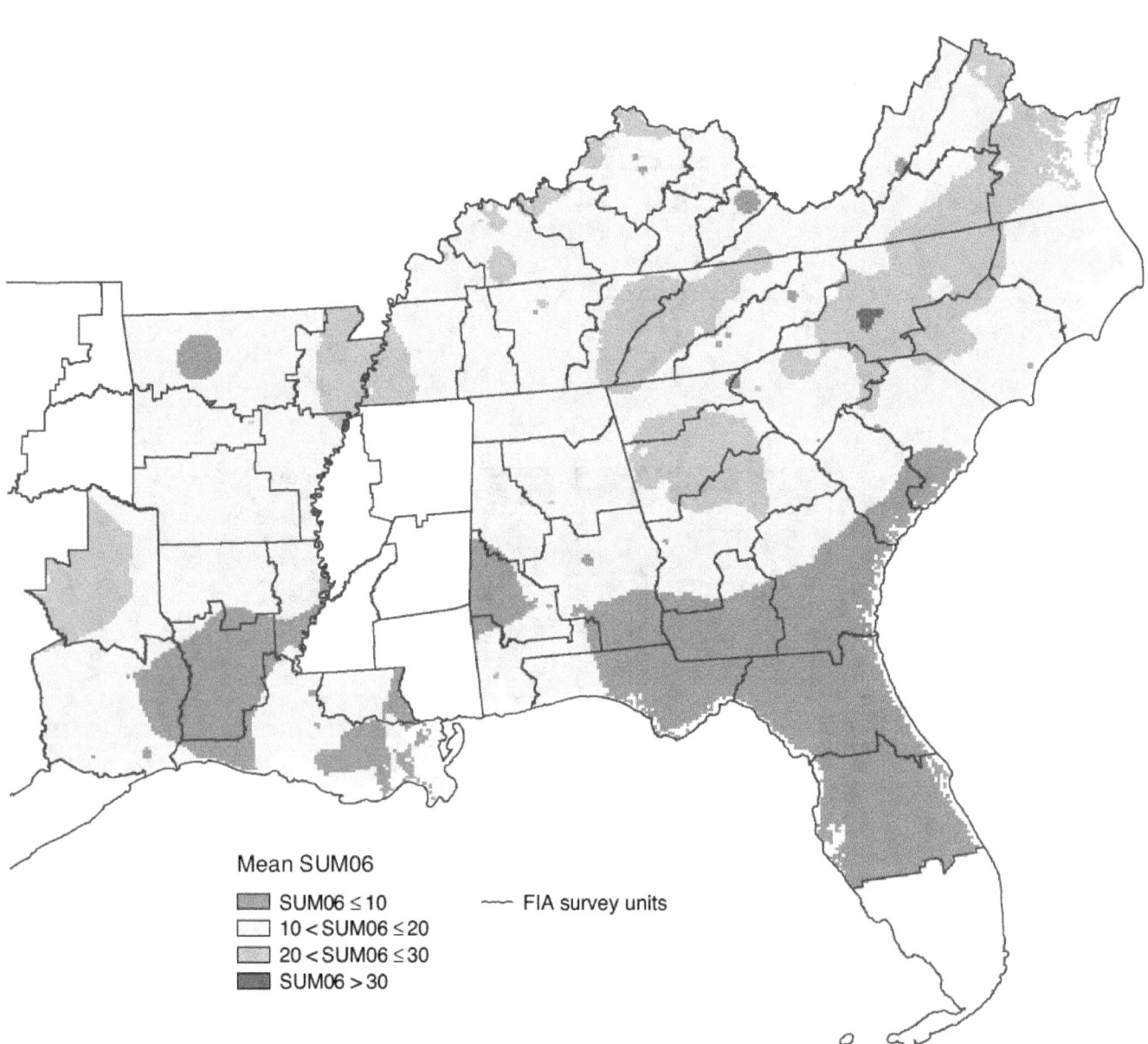

Mean SUM06

- SUM06 ≤ 10
- 10 < SUM06 ≤ 20
- 20 < SUM06 ≤ 30
- SUM06 > 30

‒‒‒ FIA survey units

Figure 11—Average 3-month growing season SUM06 values for the study area, 2002–06.

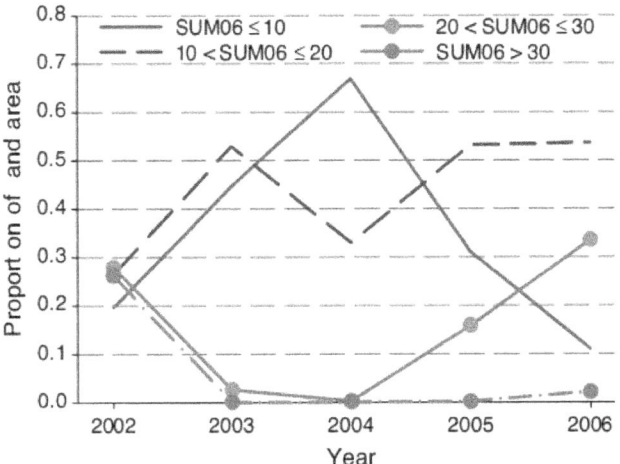

Figure 12—The proportion of land area in each SUM06 category by year.

Moisture Index

On average, from 2002 to 2006, most of the land area in the South was classified as having a moisture deficit (MI ≤ -0.15) during the 3-month (June, July, and August) growing season (fig. 13). However, during this time period, moisture balance or surplus (MI > -0.15) was observed along the Atlantic Coastal Plain and in the Southern Appalachians. There also was temporal variation in the MI from 2002 to 2006. The driest growing seasons were observed in 2002 and 2006, where about 80 percent of the land area was classified as having a moisture deficit (fig. 14). The greatest proportion of land (about 0.27) with a moisture surplus (MI > 0.15) occurred in 2003.

Integration of Injury, Exposure, and Moisture

Across years, biosites where injury was observed generally had a higher MI value and a higher SUM06 value. The average SUM06 value for biosites where injury was not observed was 12.85 ppm-hours while biosites where injury was observed was 13.47 ppm-hours (but this difference was not significant). The average MI for biosites where injury was not observed was -0.198 (moisture deficit category) while the average MI was -0.082 (approximate moisture

balance) for biosites where injury was observed. The null hypothesis for the Hotelling T^2 test was rejected ($p < 0.001$) and we provisionally accepted the alternative hypothesis that there was a difference between mean response vectors for biosites where injury was observed versus biosites where injury was not observed. We then examined the simultaneous 95 percent Bonferroni confidence intervals to identify whether a single variable was significant. Because the 95 percent Bonferroni confidence intervals for the MI did not contain zero, the MI contributed significantly toward explaining the difference between mean response vectors (fig. 15). The highest percentage of biosites with injury occurred in 2003, the only year when SUM06 values were > 10 ppm-hours on over 50 percent of the land area and nearly 75 percent of the land area was in a moisture surplus or balance. In contrast, the year 2002, which had the second highest amount of injury, was a rather dry year, with about 80 percent of the land area having a moisture deficit. However, this was the only year where almost 30 percent of the land area saw exposures between 20 and 30 ppm-hours, and another 26 percent had SUM06 values > 30 ppm-hours. Even in years with relatively low ozone exposure, as in 2004 (SUM06 values on nearly 70 percent of the land area were < 10 ppm-hours), the high degree of moisture surplus and balance likely contributed to 17 percent of sites having injury.

Risk Assessment

Overall, about 163.0 million acres of forest land (90 percent) in the South was classified in the no risk category (BI < 5) (table 8). The lowest risk category also contained about 90 percent of the tree volume in the South (table 9). The average BI for sensitive species was < 5, which indicates that there was not a potential regional ozone issue for a particular sensitive species. While most of the forest land in the South had no risk of ozone injury, 17.5 million acres of forest land were classified in the low (BI 5–14.9), moderate (BI 15–24.9), and high (BI ≥ 25) risk categories (table 8). Within the low, moderate, and high risk forest areas, about 20.3 billion cubic feet of tree volume was from sensitive species (table 9). The area at greatest risk from ozone injury occurred in northern Georgia (fig. 16) where about 21,914 acres of forest were classified in the high-risk category (table 8). Within this high risk area moderately sensitive and sensitive species accounted for about 58 percent of the tree volume.

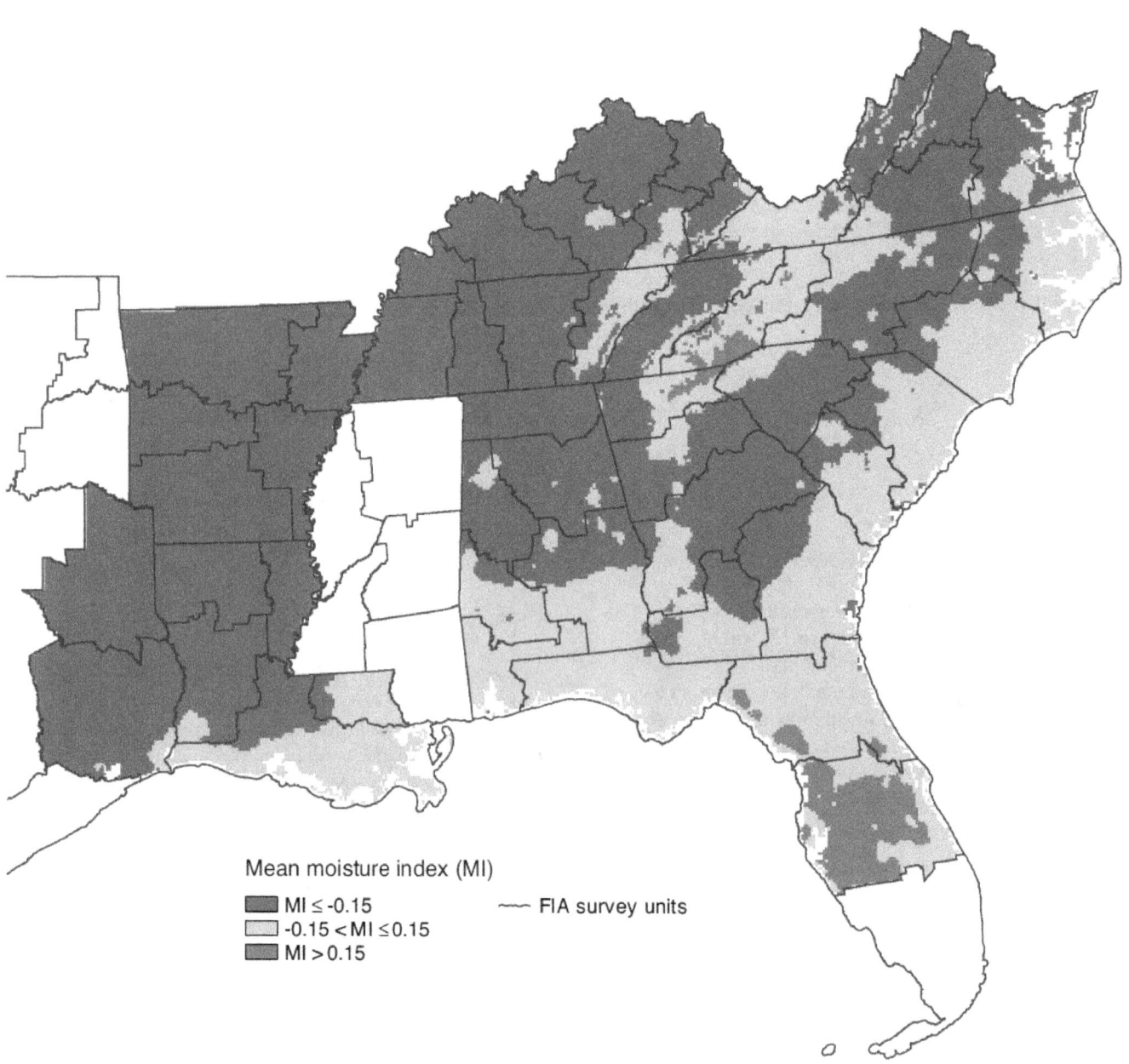

Figure 13—Average 3-month growing season moisture index for the study area, 2002–06.

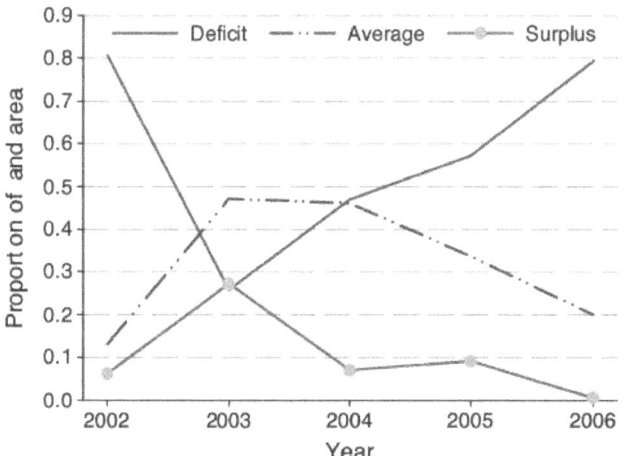

Figure 14—The proportion of land area in each moisture index category by year.

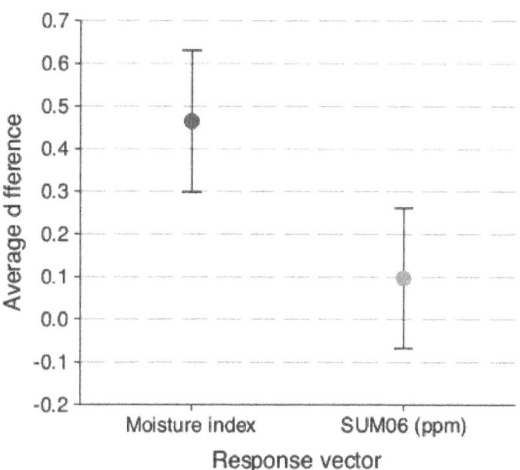

Figure 15—The average difference between biosites with and without injury by response vector. Ninety-five percent Bonferroni simultaneous confidence intervals are indicated by the vertical lines.

Table 8—Estimated area of forest land by biosite index and risk category by State, 2002–06

State	Biosite index[a]			
	0 to 4.9 (no risk)	5.0 to 14.9 (low risk)	15.0 to 24.9 (moderate risk)	≥ 25 (high risk)
	acres			
Alabama	22,566,073	0	0	0
Arkansas	18,271,773	131,880	0	0
Florida	15,037,406	0	0	0
Georgia	19,228,395	5,426,306	262,482	21,914
Kentucky	11,822,577	307,210	0	0
Louisiana[b]	14,138,135	0	0	0
North Carolina	16,980,241	1,615,518	0	0
South Carolina	3,551,265	9,342,953	0	0
Tennessee	13,936,824	14,807	0	0
Texas	12,129,663	0	0	0
Virginia	15,337,078	421,312	0	0
Total	162,999,432	17,259,984	262,482	21,914

[a] Biosite index based on interpolated values for each Forest Inventory and Analysis plot.

[b] 2002–05.

Table 9—Estimated volume of live trees, by biosite index and risk category, by State, and ozone-sensitivity category, 2002–06

State and ozone-sensitivity category[a]	Biosite index[b]			
	0 to 4.9 (no risk)	5.0 to 14.9 (low risk)	15.0 to 24.9 (moderate risk)	≥ 25 (high risk)
	million cubic feet			
Alabama				
Unknown	11,649.53			
Insensitive	1,714.17			
Moderately sensitive	2,434.30			
Sensitive	16,558.33			
Arkansas				
Unknown	9,292.95	286.90		
Insensitive	3,722.19	4.04		
Moderately sensitive	5,051.03	5.43		
Sensitive	9,226.22	71.60		
Florida				
Unknown	15,487.38			
Insensitive	28.98			
Moderately sensitive	105.08			
Sensitive	3,169.31			
Georgia				
Unknown	14,030.55	2,069.44	98.97	10.89
Insensitive	919.07	1,001.77	55.26	10.06
Moderately sensitive	1,279.41	1,082.25	46.99	1.19
Sensitive	11,950.25	6,290.49	328.15	27.46
Kentucky				
Unknown	7,667.04	217.73		
Insensitive	5,015.92	99.49		
Moderately sensitive	2,611.13	25.13		
Sensitive	6,832.82	167.84		
Louisiana[c]				
Unknown	10,560.39			
Insensitive	505.21			
Moderately sensitive	867.64			
Sensitive	10,404.32			
North Carolina				
Unknown	8,499.58	709.82		
Insensitive	3,802.02	169.97		
Moderately sensitive	2,369.76	258.16		
Sensitive	19,423.72	1,426.90		
South Carolina				
Unknown	2,393.20	4,184.45		
Insensitive	153.24	893.06		
Moderately sensitive	191.47	753.31		
Sensitive	3,818.57	9,298.64		
Tennessee				
Unknown	10,087.02	8.74		
Insensitive	5,393.14	4.10		
Moderately sensitive	3,410.90	4.97		
Sensitive	9,241.75	18.12		

continued

Table 9—Estimated volume of live trees, by biosite index and risk category, by State, and ozone-sensitivity category, 2002–06 (continued)

State and ozone-sensitivity category[a]	Biosite index[b]			
	0 to 4.9 (no risk)	5.0 to 14.9 (low risk)	15.0 to 24.9 (moderate risk)	≥25 (high risk)
	million cubic feet			
Texas				
Unknown	6,099.80			
Insensitive	397.55			
Moderately sensitive	1,776.17			
Sensitive	9,280.33			
Virginia				
Unknown	7,216.67	308.49		
Insensitive	5,220.88	262.50		
Moderately sensitive	2,888.90	109.95		
Sensitive	15,726.05	435.24		
All States				
Unknown	102,984.12	7,785.58	98.97	10.89
Insensitive	26,872.37	2,434.93	55.26	10.06
Moderately sensitive	22,985.79	2,239.18	46.99	1.19
Sensitive	115,631.67	17,708.82	328.15	27.46
Total	268,473.95	30,168.52	529.37	49.60

[a] Ozone-sensitivity categories are based on both field observations and fumigation trials (Smith and others 2007).

[b] Biosite index based on interpolated values for each Forest Inventory and Analysis plot.

[c] 2002–05.

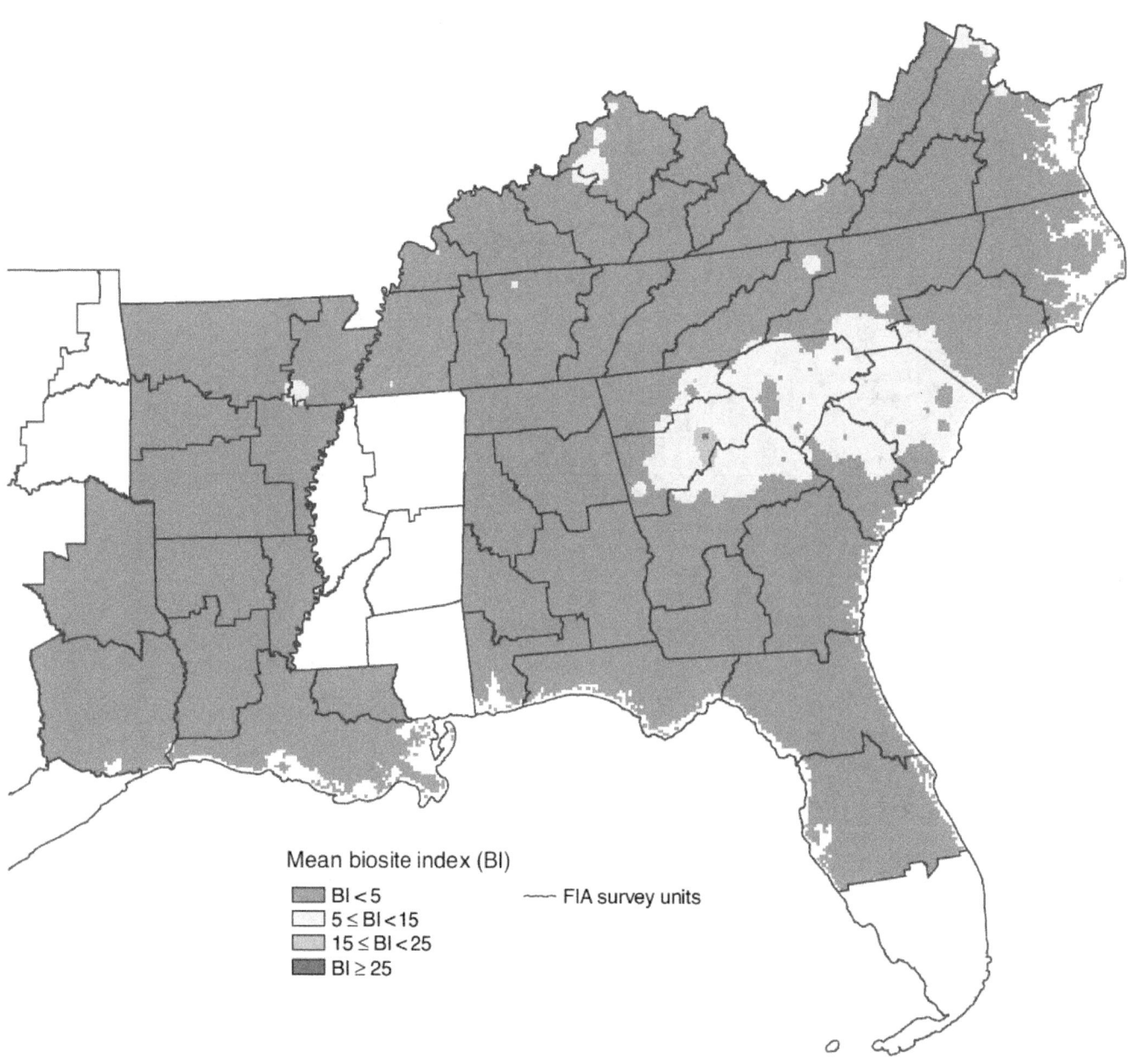

Mean biosite index (BI)

BI < 5
5 ≤ BI < 15
15 ≤ BI < 25
BI ≥ 25

FIA survey units

Figure 16—Average biosite index for the study area, 2002–06.

Discussion

The U.S. Environmental Protection Agency (2008) has reported a general decline of 13 percent in levels of ambient ozone across the South over the past 10 years, but, this decline has been spatially variable. Kentucky, Tennessee, and North Carolina had ozone declines between 12 and 16 percent while South Carolina and Georgia only had declines of 4 and 9 percent, respectively. Despite overall declines in ambient ozone concentrations, ozone induced foliar injury still occurs in the South, particularly in Georgia and South Carolina.

The incidence of foliar injury varied both spatially and temporally. When the amount and severity of injury recorded on biosites was averaged across all 5 years, most of the forest area in the South was classified in the low or no risk category (table 8). While this seems to indicate that there is not currently a regional ozone forest health issue, this is complicated by the fact that a majority of the South was in a moisture deficit during the 2002-06 time period. There was an area of relatively high risk identified in northern Georgia. This area may be a candidate for a followup investigation to determine whether there is an actual forest health issue. While South Carolina did not stand out as being at particularly high risk for ozone injury, only 28 percent of the forest land in that State was in the no risk category, the lowest for any State. In addition, for 2002 through 2006, 40 percent of the 10 highest BI values in the South were in South Carolina. These consistent low to moderate levels of injury occurring year after year warrant continued monitoring and close scrutiny for potential forest health impacts. Further research is also needed to relate foliar injury to responses at individual tree species, ecosystem, and regional levels.

Numerous studies describe the importance of moisture availability in determining whether ozone injury occurs (see for example, Davis and Orendovici 2006, Smith and others 2003). In fact, the importance of spatial and interannual moisture availability may explain why strong relationships between ozone exposure and injury have not been documented in the Southern United States (Chappelka and Samuelson 1998). From the integrated analysis, (Integration of Injury, Exposure, and Moisture section) we infer that ozone exposures in the South are generally high enough to injure bioindicator plants and it is the co-occurrence of sufficient moisture availability that is actually a more important driver in determining whether injury occurs. This theory is supported by our findings that ozone exposure did not differ significantly between biosites with injury and those without, while both moisture alone and the interaction of ozone exposure and moisture did differ significantly. It appears, therefore, that ozone levels were uniformly high enough that they lacked explanatory power and, on average, biosites with injury had a moisture balance rather than a moisture deficit. One area of further research is to examine the relationship between injury severity on biosites and ozone exposure metrics under moisture balance conditions.

FIA conducts the only annual nationwide systematic survey for ozone-induced foliar injury. This information is particularly valuable to researchers studying trends in ozone exposure and injury, as well as to those assessing ozone impacts to vegetation across the United States. It is also a useful resource for government agencies, land managers, and the public as we attempt to address air quality issues that impact the natural resources of the Nation.

Acknowledgments

Of vital importance to the ozone biomonitoring program are the forest agencies for the Southern States, the State coordinators, regional trainers, field crews, and quality assurance staff who collect and verify the ozone data. The ozone biomonitoring program would not be possible without their commitment to the collection of quality data. The authors would also like to thank Stan Zarnoch, Gretchen Smith, Sally Campbell, and Sarah Jovan for their helpful comments on an earlier draft of this publication.

Literature Cited

Akin, W.E. 1991. Global patterns: climate, vegetation, and soils. Norman, OK: University of Oklahoma Press. 370 p.

Anderson, R.L.; Brown, H.D.; Chevone, B.I.; McCartney, T.C. 1988. Occurrence of air pollution symptoms (needle tip necrosis and chlorotic mottling) on eastern white pine in the Southern Appalachian Mountains. Plant Disease. 72: 130–132.

Arbaugh, M.J.; Miller, P.R.; Carroll, J.J. [and others]. 1998. Relationships of ozone exposure to pine injury in the Sierra Nevada and San Bernardino Mountains of California, USA. Environmental Pollution. 101: 291–301.

Barbo, D.N.; Chappelka, A.H.; Somers, G.L. [and others]. 1998. Diversity of an early successional plant community as influenced by ozone. New Phytologist. 138: 653–662.

Bartholomay, G.A.; Eckert, R.T.; Smith, K.T. 1997. Reductions in tree-ring widths of white pine following ozone exposure at Acadia National Park, Maine, U.S.A. Canadian Journal of Forest Research. 27: 361–368.

Bechtold, W.A.; Patterson, P.L., eds. 2005. The enhanced forest inventory and analysis program--national sampling design and estimation procedures. Gen. Tech. Rep. SRS–80. Asheville, NC: U.S. Department of Agriculture Forest Service, Southern Research Station. 85 p.

Benoit, L.F.; Skelly, J.M.; Moore, L.D.; Dochinger, L.S. 1982. Radial growth reductions of *Pinus strobus* L. correlated with foliar ozone sensitivity as an indicator of ozone induced losses in eastern forests. Canadian Journal of Forest Research. 12: 673–678.

Bytnerowicz, A. 2002. Physiological/ecological interactions between ozone and nitrogen deposition in forest ecosystems. Phyton - Annales Rei Botanicae. 42: 13–28.

Chappelka, A.H.; Samuelson, L.J. 1998. Ambient ozone effects on forest trees of the Eastern United States: a review. New Phytologist. 139(1): 91–108.

Coulston, J.W.; Riitters, K.H. 2005. Preserving biodiversity under current and future climates: a case study. Global Ecology and Biogeography. 14(1): 31–38.

Coulston, J.W.; Smith, G.C.; Smith, W.D. 2003. Regional assessment of ozone sensitive tree species using bioindicator plants. Environmental Monitoring and Assessment. 83: 113–127.

Daly, C.; Gibson, W.P.; Taylor, G.H. [and others]. 2002. A knowledge-based approach to the statistical mapping of climate. Climate Research. 22: 99–113.

Davis, D.D.; Orendovici, T. 2006. Incidence of ozone symptoms on vegetation within a National Wildlife Refuge in New Jersey, USA. Environmental Pollution. 143: 555–564.

Fredericksen, T.S.; Joyce, B.J.; Skelly, J.M. [and others]. 1995. Physiology, morphology, and ozone uptake of leaves of black cherry seedlings, saplings, and canopy trees. Environmental Pollution. 89(3): 273–283.

Hildebrand, E.; Skelly, J.M.; Fredericksen, T.S. 1996. Foliar response of ozone-sensitive hardwood tree species from 1991 to 1993 in the Shenandoah National Park, Virginia. Canadian Journal of Forest Research. 26: 658–669.

Johnson, R.A.; Wichern, D.W. 2002. Applied Multivariate Statistical Analysis, 5th ed. New Jersey: Prentice Hall. 767 p.

Karnosky, D.F.; Skelly, J.M.; Percy, K.E.; Chappelka, A.H. 2007. Perspectives regarding 50 years of research on effects of tropospheric ozone air pollution on U.S. forests. Environmental Pollution. 147(3): 489–506.

Koch, F.H.; Coulston, J.W.; Smith, W.D. [In press]. High-resolution mapping of drought conditions. In: Potter, K.M.; Conkling B.L. eds. Forest health monitoring 2008 national technical report. Gen. Tech. Rep. Asheville, NC: U.S. Department of Agriculture Forest Service, Southern Research Station.

Little, E.L., Jr. 1979. Checklist of United States trees (native and naturalized). Agric. Handb. 541. Washington, DC: U.S. Department of Agriculture. 375 p.

McLaughlin, S.B.; Downing, D.J. 1996. Interactive effects of ambient ozone and climate measured on growth of mature loblolly pine trees. Canadian Journal of Forest Research. 26: 670–681.

Patterson, M.C.; Samuelson, L.J.; Somers, G.; Mays, P.A. 2000. Environmental control of ozone uptake in forest trees of the Great Smoky Mountains National Park. Environmental Pollution. 110: 225–233.

Peterson, D.L.; Arbaugh, M.J.; Robinson, L.J. 1993. Effects of ozone and climate on ponderosa pine (*Pinus ponderosa*) growth in the Colorado Rocky Mountains. Canadian Journal of Forest Research. 23: 1750–1759.

Rebbeck, J. 1996. Chronic ozone effects on three northeastern hardwood species: growth and biomass. Canadian Journal of Forest Research. 26: 1788–1798.

Reinert, R.A.; Shafer, S.R.; Eason, G. [and others]. 1996. Responses of loblolly pine to ozone and simulated acidic rain. Canadian Journal of Forest Research. 26: 1715–1723.

Samuelson, L.J.; Edwards, G.S. 1993. A comparison of sensitivity to ozone in seedlings and trees of *Quercus rubra* L. New Phytologist. 125(2): 373–379.

Samuelson, L.; Kelly, J.M. 2001. Scaling ozone effects from seedlings to forest trees. New Phytologist. 149(1): 21–41.

Smith, G.; Coulston, J.; Jepsen, E.; Prichard, T. 2003. A national ozone biomonitoring program - results from field surveys of ozone sensitive plants in northeastern forests (1994–2000). Environmental Monitoring and Assessment. 87(3): 271–291.

Smith, G.C.; Smith, W.D.; Coulston, J.W. 2007. Ozone bioindicator sampling and estimation. Gen. Tech. Rep. NRS–20. Newtown Square, PA: U.S. Department of Agriculture Forest Service, Northern Research Station. 34 p.

Somers, G.L.; Chappelka, A.H.; Rosseau, P.; Renfro, J.R. 1998. Empirical evidence of growth decline related to visible ozone injury. Forest Ecology and Management. 104: 129–137.

The H. John Heinz III Center for Science, Economics, and the Environment. 2008. The state of the Nation's ecosystems 2008: Measuring the land, waters, and living resources of the United States. Washington, DC: Island Press. 368 p.

Thornthwaite, C.W. 1948. An approach towards a rational classification of climate. Geographical Review. 38(1): 55–94.

U.S. Department of Agriculture Forest Service. 2004. Forest inventory and analysis national core field guide: field data collection procedures for phase 3 plots. Version 2.0. Washington, DC. 164 p. Vol. II. Internal report. On file with: U.S. Department of Agriculture Forest Service, Forest Inventory and Analysis, 201 14th St., Washington, DC 20250.

U.S. Department of Agriculture Natural Resources Conservation Service. 2006. The PLANTS database. Baton Rouge, LA: National Plant Data Center. http://plants.usda.gov. [Date accessed unknown].

U.S. Environmental Protection Agency. 2004. The ozone report: measuring progress through 2003. EPA 454/K–04–001. Research Triangle Park, NC: U.S. Environmental Protection Agency, Office of Air Quality Planning and Standards Emissions, Monitoring, and Analysis Division. 19 p.

U.S. Environmental Protection Agency. 2008. Weather makes a difference: 8-hour ozone trends for 1997–2007. State and local information for EPA region 4. http://www.epa.gov/air/airtrends/weather.html. [Date accessed: August 26].

Willmott, C.J.; Feddema, J.J. 1992. A more rational climatic moisture index. The Professional Geographer. 44(1): 84–88.